DATE DUE			

ACID RAIN

© Aladdin Books Ltd 1990

First published in
the United States in 1990 by
Gloucester Press
387 Park Avenue South
New York NY 10016

Printed in Belgium

The publishers would like to
acknowledge that the
photographs reproduced within
this book have been posed by
models or have been obtained
from photographic agencies.

Design	David West Children's Book Design
Editor	Elise Bradbury
Picture research	Cecilia Weston-Baker
Illustrator	Ian Moores

The author: Dr. Tony Hare is a
writer, ecologist and TV
presenter. He works with several
environmental organizations,
including the London Wildlife
Trust, the British Association of
Nature Conservations, and
Plantlife, of which he is Chairman
of the Board.

The consultants: Jacky Karas is a
Senior Research Associate at the
Climatic Research Unit at the
University of East Anglia.

Chris Rose is Director of Media
Natura, an organization that
brings together conservation
groups and the media. He also
acts as a consultant to
Greenpeace and the Worldwide
Fund for Nature.

Library of Congress Cataloging-in-Publication Data

Hare, Tony.
    Acid rain / Tony Hare.
        p. cm. -- (Save our Earth)
    Summary: Examines the cause and effects of
acid rain, and shows how it can be prevented.
    ISBN 0-531-17247-3
    1. Acid rain--Environmental aspects--Juvenile
literature. 2. Pollution--Juvenile literature.
[1. Acid rain. 2. Pollution.] I. Title. II. Series.
TD195.44.H37   1990
363.73'86--dc20   90-3228 CIP AC

SAVE OUR EARTH

TONY HARE

GLOUCESTER PRESS

London · New York · Toronto · Sydney

CONTENTS

INTRODUCTION

Rain is very important to us. All living things need water to survive, including us and the crops we grow. Rain supplies us with the water we need. But this life-giving rain is now being poisoned by pollution in the air. This pollution comes mainly from the fuels burned in cars, homes, factories, and power stations, and combines with moisture in the atmosphere to make acids, and then falls to the ground with the rain. Polluted rain threatens people's health, destroys life in ponds, lakes and rivers, harms and kills trees and damages buildings. It is called acid rain. We can stop acid rain by making our homes, factories and power stations cleaner, and by improving our cars and using them less. However, we need to act quickly, because the problem of acid rain is worsening.

◀ **Rain fills our lakes, reservoirs, and rivers, supplying the water we use and drink. It also waters our crops, allowing us to grow enough food for ourselves, and for the animals we raise for meat and milk. In the deserts of the world, where there is little rain, life is a constant struggle against drought and hunger.**

AIR POLLUTION

When poisonous, dirty or harmful substances get into the air it is said to be polluted. There are lots of different types of air pollution. Industry's waste products are emitted into the air from factories. Pesticides drift across the land and are carried through the air when farmers spray them onto crops. Animal waste from farms with large numbers of animals produces gases which cause air pollution. Power stations burn coal, natural gas, and oil, and the smoke and fumes rise from their chimneys into the atmosphere. Cars, trucks, trains and buses burn gasoline or diesel and belch out their exhaust gases.

Acid rain is caused by some of these types of pollution, particularly that from power stations and motor vehicles. It is one of the most serious and threatening results of air pollution because it causes long-term damage to people and the environment.

▼▶ **Air pollution comes from many different sources. The pictures below show some of the producers of substances which pollute the air. Air pollution is sometimes bad enough to be seen – for example in cities like Rio de Janeiro (right), where exhaust fumes from large numbers of motor vehicles are one factor in producing smog.**

Home fire

Factory

Factory farm

Vehicle exhausts

Power station

**Fertilizer
spray**

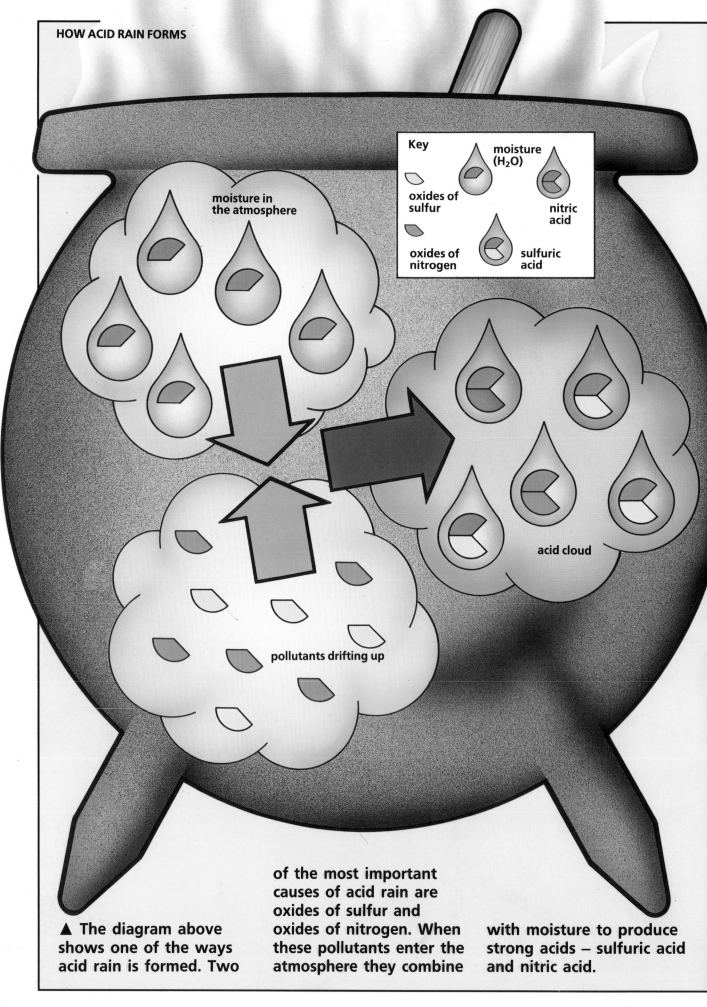

moisture in
the atmosphere

Key

moisture
(H₂O)

oxides of
sulfur

nitric
acid

oxides of
nitrogen

sulfuric
acid

acid cloud

pollutants drifting up

▲ The diagram above shows one of the ways acid rain is formed. Two of the most important causes of acid rain are oxides of sulfur and oxides of nitrogen. When these pollutants enter the atmosphere they combine with moisture to produce strong acids – sulfuric acid and nitric acid.

WHAT IS ACID RAIN?

Litmus paper

Liquid

Liquids like lemon juice and vinegar taste sharp; this sharpness is called acidity, and these liquids are known as acids. Distilled water is known as neutral; it is not acidic at all. Normal rainwater is slightly acidic. But in severely polluted areas acid rain can be as acidic or even more acidic than lemon juice or vinegar.

When strong acids are introduced into natural environments they can cause great damage to plants, animals and people. These acids can also gradually eat away buildings and other materials.

The oxides of sulfur and nitrogen that combine with water to make acid rain are mainly produced when fuels are burned. Sulfur exists naturally in coal, oil and gas, which produce sulfur oxides. Nitrogen occurs in fuels and the atmosphere, and also evaporates from agricultural fertilizers. Despite its name, acid rain is not always wet. The chemicals that combine to create it can also result in an invisible, dry dust which falls locally and is just as bad for the environment.

▲ It is possible to carry out a simple experiment to test how acidic the rain is by using litmus paper. The more acid in the rain, the darker red the paper becomes when it is dipped into a sample of the rainwater.

▼ Power stations are one main source of the chemicals that cause acid rain. As they burn fuel, pollution pours from their chimneys, including sulfur oxides and nitrogen oxides. Some of the pollution falls nearby as dry deposition. The rest drifts upward and combines with moisture to form acid, which then falls as acid rain.

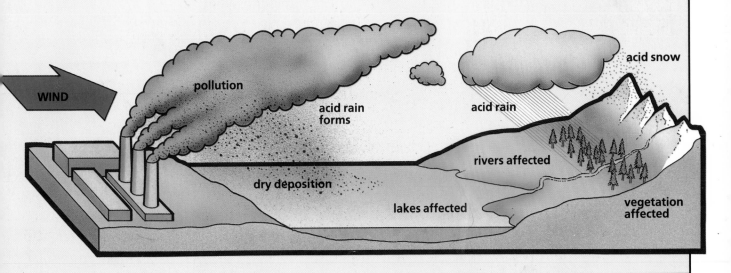

WIND

pollution

acid rain forms

acid snow

acid rain

dry deposition

rivers affected

lakes affected

vegetation affected

INCREASING ACIDITY

In the last century, people began to realize that the filth pumped out from the increasing number of chimneys of homes and factories was leading to pollution of the rain. Even before this, people had complained that the smoke from chimneys created an unpleasant environment. Thus it is probable that acid rain has existed as a result of human activity for hundreds of years.

Acid rain can occur naturally. Volcanoes, swamps and rotting plants produce sulfur dioxide, one of the oxides of sulfur, so they participate in forming a natural kind of acid rain. Natural acid rain is just as damaging to the environment, but it occurs in much smaller quantities than the acid rain caused by human-made pollution.

Between the 1950s and the 1970s the rain over Europe increased in acidity by about 10 times. Acidity decreased during the 1980s, but although many countries have begun to act against the pollution that causes acid rain, the problem is not going away.

▼ Harmful substances in the environment do not get there only as a result of human activities. Sulfur dioxide, for example, is produced when volcanoes erupt. Worldwide, natural sources may produce one half of all acid pollution. But in industrial areas, up to 90 percent of sulfur dioxide may come from human-made sources.

Unnatural 90%

Natural 10%

Burning fuels produces sulfur dioxide and oxides of nitrogen.

Industry

Cars

Power station

Domestic

Power stations, home heating systems, cars, and industries all use fuel.

A WORLDWIDE PROBLEM

One of the major problems with acid rain is that it gets carried from the places where it is produced to other areas. Tall chimneys, built to ensure that pollution from dirty industries is carried away from nearby cities, lift the pollution into the atmosphere. When it gets picked up by the moisture in the air it forms acids, which become part of the clouds. These clouds get carried off by the wind, often ending up long distances from where they formed. Eventually the acids come down with the rain, usually two or three days later.

Pollution sometimes creates acid rain which falls near the area where it is produced. For example, in Britain, Scotland suffers from acid rain produced by English factories. However, often the pollution is exported from one country to another; for instance, pollution from the industrial areas of Britain and other parts of Europe causes acid rain in Scandinavia.

▼ All over the world pollution is produced that leads to acid rain. The majority of acid pollution is produced by heavy industrial areas, such as Europe and North America in the northern hemisphere, and the rapidly developing industrial countries of southern Africa, South America and Asia in the southern hemisphere.

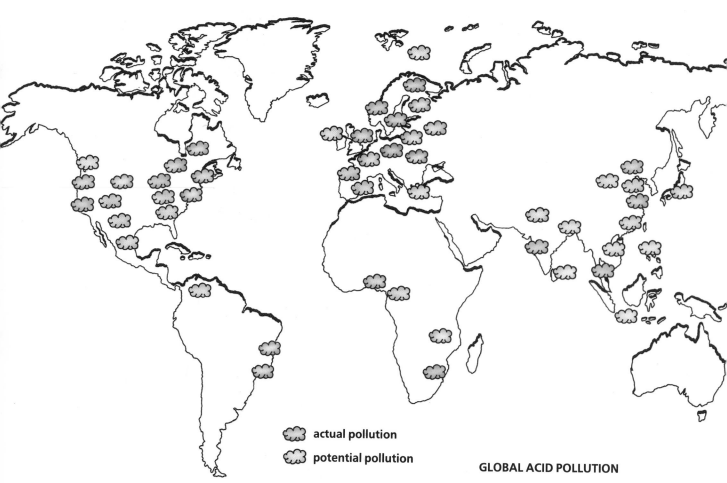

actual pollution

potential pollution

GLOBAL ACID POLLUTION

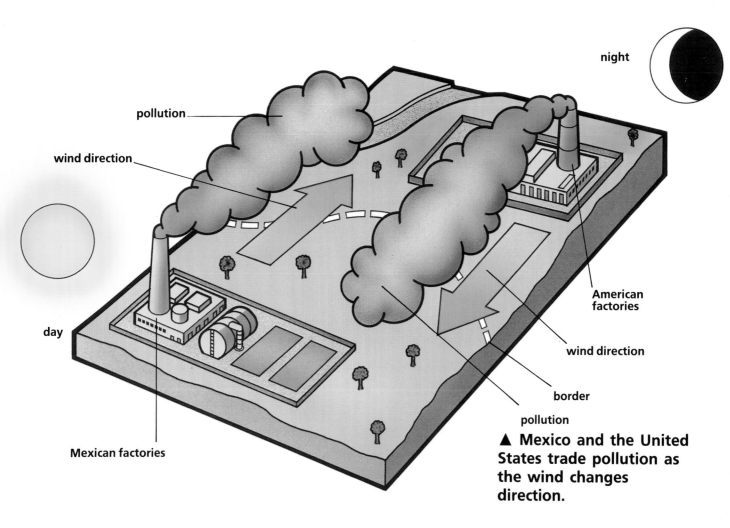

night

pollution

wind direction

day

Mexican factories

American factories

wind direction

border

pollution

▲ **Mexico and the United States trade pollution as the wind changes direction.**

As developing countries like Thailand (shown here) become industrialized, they build more roads and their cities expand. Hand in hand with this development comes a massive increase in the number of cars, which causes an increase in air pollution.

THE DEAD LAKES

Acid rain damages soil when it falls to the ground. It also has a dramatic effect on water life when it falls either directly into lakes, or drains into them off hills or from rivers and streams. The majority of wild plants and animals that live in clean, unpolluted lakes are not able to tolerate the acid water. They can also be poisoned by substances that the acid washes out of the surrounding soil into the water.

All over the world there are lakes where the wildlife has suffered badly, or has died out altogether, as a result of acid rain. Thousands of lakes in Scandinavia, for example, are without life. They have received so much acid rain over the years as a result of the wind carrying acid clouds from Britain and other countries, that almost nothing can survive in them. Since the 1930s and 1940s some Swedish lakes have increased as much as 1,000 times in acidity.

▶ Lakes that have been heavily polluted by acid rain often look clear and clean. Unfortunately they look clear because they are virtually devoid of life. Tiny plants and animals of many different types teem in unpolluted lakes. When these die off in acid lakes the water is left clear – and lifeless.

▶ An unpolluted lake is home to a web of life. Small plants and animals provide food for insects. Small fish, such as roach, eat the insects. In turn, they are eaten by larger fish such as pikes, and by birds like herons. However, once the lake begins to turn acidic the wildlife starts to die. Just a few living things can stand the acid, like the mats of weed and moss that carpet the lake bed. This seriously affects the food web as larger animals have no source of food. Also, fish are poisoned by aluminum that acid rain washes into the lake from the soil.

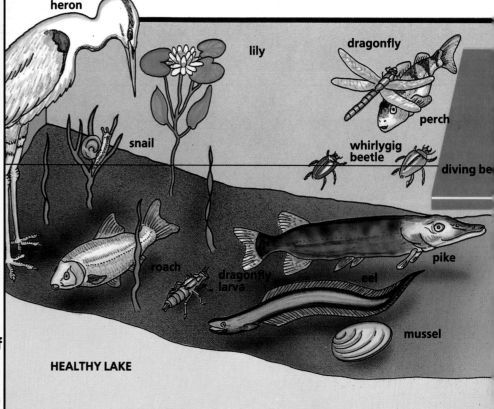

heron

lily

dragonfly

perch

snail

whirlygig beetle

diving be

roach

dragonfly larva

eel

pike

mussel

HEALTHY LAKE

dragonfly

diving
beetle

whirlygig
beetle

dragonfly larva

mat of moss and algae

ACID LAKE

DAMAGE TO TREES AND SOIL

When acid rain falls from the sky, it can affect forests as well as lakes. In many countries around the world trees are losing their leaves and becoming very thin on top. Some are dying. It is fairly certain that acid rain has been a major factor in this tree damage.

Acid rain puts trees under stress. Trees need healthy ground to grow in, and acid rain can damage soils. It interferes with the many different substances that make up the soil, upsetting their delicate balance. If the soil is harmed, the trees growing in it are less able to cope with problems like frost and drought. Once the trees are weakened by such problems, they are more susceptible to viruses, fungi, and insect pests.

Acid rain not only damages soil, but can also affect the trees directly. Sulfur dioxide can block the little pores on the leaves through which the plant takes in the air it needs to survive.

▼ **The Black Forest in West Germany was one of the first places where foresters noticed the damage to trees that has become so widespread across Europe during the last 20 years. Although this area of the Black Forest has not been badly damaged, other parts are seriously affected by acid rain. Both broad-leaved (deciduous) and conifer trees are affected.**

▼ Acid-pollution damage is the main reason why these Czechoslovakian trees lost their leaves.

▲ When trees affected by acid rain lose their leaves they sometimes try to replace them by producing short branches with new leaves on them. These are known as fear shoots.

DESTRUCTION OF BUILDINGS

When acid rain comes into contact with the materials used in buildings, statues, stained glass, paintings, and other objects, it can damage and destroy them. It slowly but surely eats them away, and the effects can be serious. Building materials crumble away, metals are corroded, the color of paint changes, leather is weakened and crusts form on the surface of glass.

In several parts of the world ancient and famous buildings are being damaged by acid rain. For instance, at London's St Paul's Cathedral in England the stonework is being eaten away by acid rain. In Washington D.C. the Washington monument and Lincoln memorial are deteriorating. India's Taj Mahal is being threatened by smoke and acid rain from oil refineries. In Rome, the Michelangelo statue of Marcus Aurelius has been removed to protect it from air pollution.

▼► Famous buildings and statues are slowly being disintegrated by acid rain. This Regency architecture in Cheltenham (below) and Polish statue (right) have both been seriously corroded by acid rain.

ACID SMOG

Air pollution from the burning of fuels such as coal can produce low-lying, dirty, smoke-infested fog, known as smog. In the past, smog used to form in many cities as a result of very dirty smoke, full of ash and other debris, from factory chimneys and homes. This kind of smog is less common now because of smokeless zones and other controls on smoke from chimneys. Nonetheless, invisible pollutants like sulfur dioxide can combine with the moisture in fog to produce a less obviously dirty, but no less dangerous, type of smog.

Vehicle exhausts can produce smog too. When sunlight hits the mixture of pollutants produced by vehicles, including hydrocarbons and oxides of nitrogen, a hazy smog is generated, called photochemical smog. Ozone forms in this smog, and so do other chemicals which are bad for people and the environment, including peroxyacetyl nitrate, which irritates the lungs and eyes.

◄ **Ozone is a colorless gas. High in the atmosphere it forms a layer which filters out the most dangerous radiation from the Sun, making life on Earth possible. However, ozone also occurs at ground level, in photochemical smog, like in this city on the border of Mexico and America. At ground level ozone is a dangerous form of pollution. Unfortunately, low-level ozone generally does not drift up to reinforce the ozone layer, which is under threat from other forms of pollution, especially CFCs, (chlorofluorocarbons), which come from aerosols and refrigerators.**

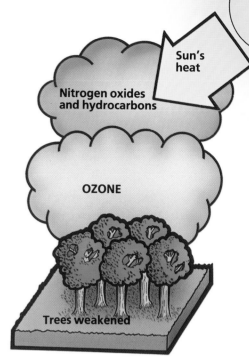

◄▲ Ozone pollution can damage the leaves of plants. All kinds of plants are at risk; fruit and vegetables as well as all types of trees. Ozone also aids the formation of acid rain, because it helps oxides of sulfur turn into sulfuric acid.

In the past, many cities suffered from smog. In London, for example, thousands of people died in smogs like this one by inhaling poisonous air; 4,000 died in 1952, the year this picture was taken. Following the pollution problems of the 1950s, the Clean Air Act was introduced to control air pollution, and London's air became much cleaner. If strict laws are passed and enforced, pollution can be successfully controlled.

BREATHING ACID

Acid rain, and the other types of pollution that go with it (acid snow, acid smog, dry deposition, and low-level ozone), harms people as well as the environment. Breathing in the acid from smog or dry deposition can cause breathing problems. Low-level ozone can also cause coughing and breathing difficulties, and sometimes causes irritation to the eyes, nose and throat. People with asthma are particularly vulnerable to the effects of pollution.

Dust, gas, and particles may have potentially cancerous chemicals associated with them. The black sooty particles produced by diesel vehicles in particular, contain cancer-causing chemicals. Acid rain can wash aluminum into the water supply. Tests have suggested that in certain cases aluminum may be one cause of Alzheimer's disease, the illness that makes elderly people forgetful and unable to concentrate.

◄► Many cities have such bad air pollution that people who spend time outside, such as traffic policemen and bicyclists, have to wear antipollution masks. In some places, newspapers and radio and television stations issue daily pollution bulletins. People especially at risk, like asthma sufferers, elderly and very young people, and pregnant women, are advised to avoid exercise during alerts.

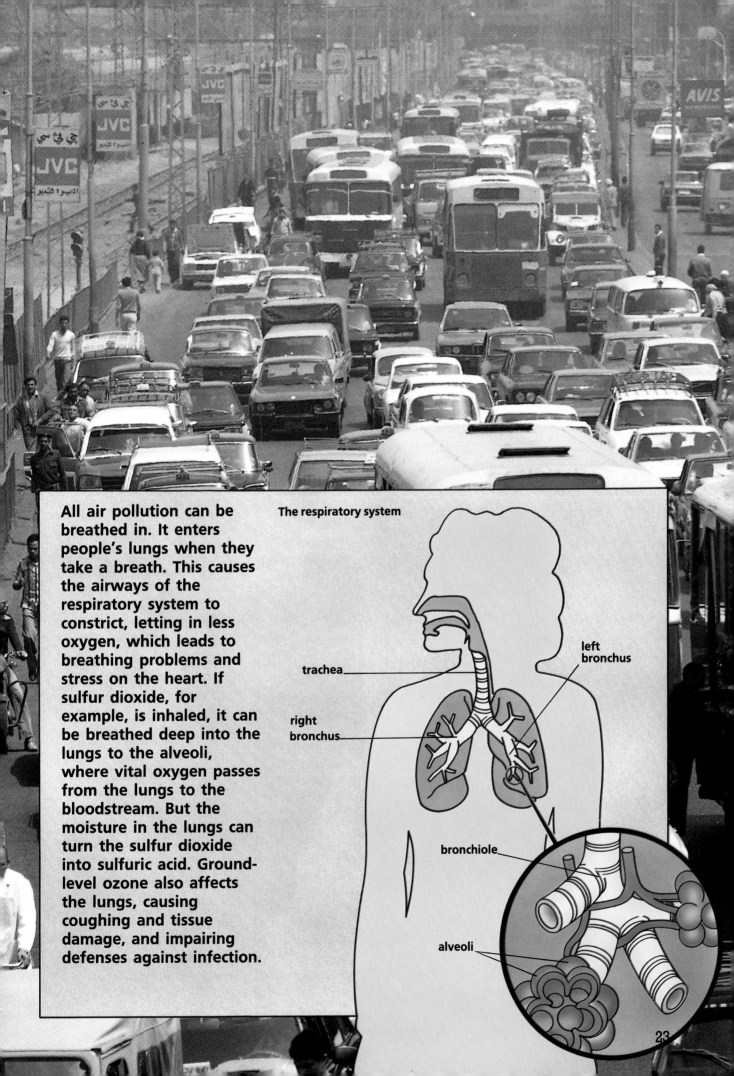

All air pollution can be breathed in. It enters people's lungs when they take a breath. This causes the airways of the respiratory system to constrict, letting in less oxygen, which leads to breathing problems and stress on the heart. If sulfur dioxide, for example, is inhaled, it can be breathed deep into the lungs to the alveoli, where vital oxygen passes from the lungs to the bloodstream. But the moisture in the lungs can turn the sulfur dioxide into sulfuric acid. Ground-level ozone also affects the lungs, causing coughing and tissue damage, and impairing defenses against infection.

The respiratory system

trachea

right bronchus

left bronchus

bronchiole

alveoli

23

WHAT CAN BE DONE?

The problem of acid rain can be tackled. Cleaning up smoke from factories and homes in recent decades has helped, but more measures need to be taken to solve the problem of acid rain. These measures include:

● Cleaning up pollution from power stations.

● Cleaning up car exhausts. Many countries have introduced 3-way catalytic converters, which are fitted to car exhausts and cut out 90 percent of the oxides of nitrogen (and also cut some other pollutants).

● Restricting the use of motor vehicles, increasing the use of public transportation and using alternative forms of transportation, such as bicycles.

● Conserving energy by using it efficiently in homes and factories, and researching and introducing alternative forms of energy like wind and solar power.

● Increasing regulations on pollution production and improving enforcement of these rules.

The acid pollution problem is not just a local one, restricted to particular countries. It is a global problem – at the moment it is especially important in Europe and North America, where many people, like these Greenpeace demonstrators, have protested about it. In the years to come acid rain will become increasingly serious in many parts of the world. The demand for cars in the developing countries, for example, is expected to be such that the number of cars worldwide will soon double, from one billion to two billion.

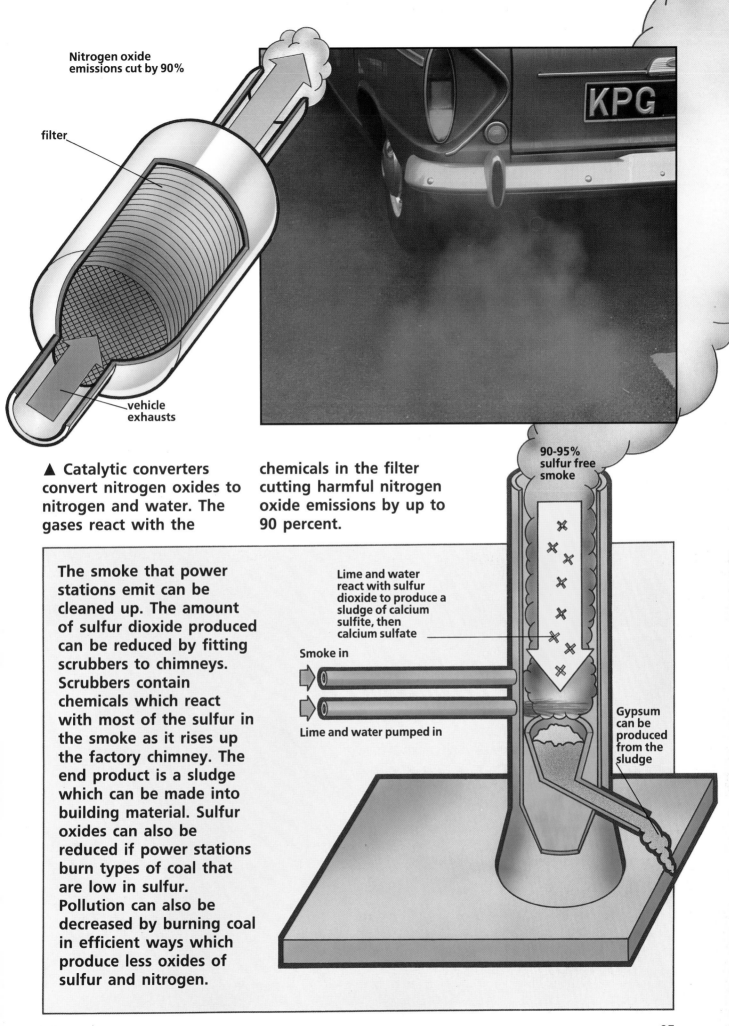

Nitrogen oxide emissions cut by 90%

filter

vehicle exhausts

▲ Catalytic converters convert nitrogen oxides to nitrogen and water. The gases react with the chemicals in the filter cutting harmful nitrogen oxide emissions by up to 90 percent.

The smoke that power stations emit can be cleaned up. The amount of sulfur dioxide produced can be reduced by fitting scrubbers to chimneys. Scrubbers contain chemicals which react with most of the sulfur in the smoke as it rises up the factory chimney. The end product is a sludge which can be made into building material. Sulfur oxides can also be reduced if power stations burn types of coal that are low in sulfur. Pollution can also be decreased by burning coal in efficient ways which produce less oxides of sulfur and nitrogen.

90-95% sulfur free smoke

Lime and water react with sulfur dioxide to produce a sludge of calcium sulfite, then calcium sulfate

Smoke in

Lime and water pumped in

Gypsum can be produced from the sludge

WHAT YOU CAN DO

Here are some things you can do to help solve the acid rain problem:

● Cut back on car use – walk to school or go by bicycle or public transportation.

● If your home is heated by a real fire that uses wood or coal, get your parents to use smokeless fuel.

● Write to your senator or congressman to ask them to pressure for more regulations against the pollution which causes acid rain.

Useful addresses

Greenpeace
1436 U. Street N.W.
Washington, D.C. 2009

Friends of the Earth
530 7th Street S.E.
Washington, D.C. 2003

Acid Rain Foundation
1630 Blackhawk Hills
St. Paul, MN 55122

Air Pollution Control Associates
P.O. Box 2861
Pittsburgh, PA 15230

Environmental Action Coalition
625 Broadway
New York, NY 10012

Chemical Manufacturer's Assocaition
2501 M Street, N.W.
Washington, D.C. 20037

Designing a poster:

One of the most important things you can do is to make more people aware of the problems caused by acid rain. One way you can do this is to make a poster to hang up on a school notice board.

1) Think up a striking or clever heading for the poster which will grab people's attention.

2) Design an illustration or symbol like the one shown here or cut pictures out of magazines and make a collage that conveys the main message.

3) Read through this book and try to summarize in about 30-40 words what is happening with acid rain and why it is important.

4) Again by reading through the book, make some suggestions as to what can be done to prevent acid rain.

5) Include some other information if there is room, such as useful addresses to contact for more information, and symbols that are printed on environment-friendly products.

ACID RAIN

GASES IN POLLUTION PRODUCED BY CARS AND FOSSIL FUEL-BURNING POWER STATIONS ARE CREATING ACID RAIN WHICH DAMAGES FORESTS, KILLS FISH AND PLANTS AND IS DANGEROUS TO US!

WHAT CAN YOU DO?

• MOTOR VEHICLES ARE MAJOR PRODUCERS OF THE CHEMICALS THAT GO TO FORM ACID RAIN. CUT BACK ON CAR USE BY WALKING OR RIDING A BICYCLE.

• BURNING COAL ALSO PRODUCES FUMES WHICH CAN FORM ACID RAIN - SWITCH TO SMOKELESS FUEL.

• CONSERVE ENERGY AS MUCH AS YOU CAN BECAUSE MOST POWER STATIONS POLLUTE THE ATMOSPHERE WITH GASES WHICH CAUSE ACID RAIN.

USEFUL ADDRESSES

FACT FILE 1

Reducing vehicle pollution

The huge amount of pollution produced by cars can easily be reduced. Public transportation minimizes pollution from car exhausts because there are more people to each vehicle, and because some types of public transportation, like this train, run on electric power. Some cities have restrictions on the number of cars going into town; in others people have to pay to take their cars into cities. In a few places, cars are banned from city centers altogether, or traffic is decreased during pollution alerts. Research is going on into very fuel-efficient cars that do many more miles per gallon than current models. Prototypes exist which can do 70-120 miles per gallon; about twice as far for the same amount of fuel as cars on the road today.

The pH scale

The pH scale shows how acidic or alkaline a substance is. The lower the pH the more acidic the substance. Vinegar, battery acid, and wine are examples of acids. Substances like milk and bleach are the opposite to acids – they are called alkalis. They have high pH. Unpolluted rain has a pH of about 5.6. Acid rain has been recorded with a pH as low as 2.4. This may not sound too bad, but for every decrease of 1 in pH, acidity increases 10 times.

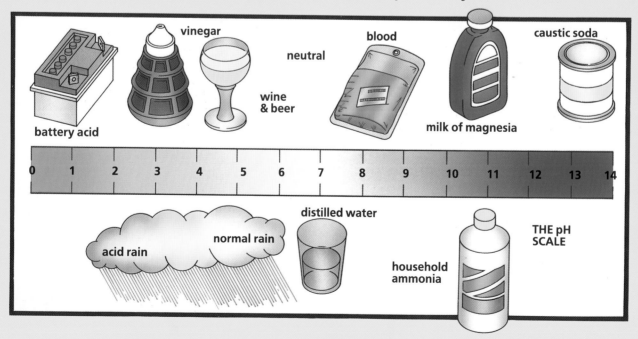

battery acid · vinegar · wine & beer · neutral · blood · milk of magnesia · caustic soda

0 1 2 3 4 5 6 7 8 9 10 11 12 13 14

acid rain · normal rain · distilled water · household ammonia · THE pH SCALE

Critical loads

Critical loads are pollution levels calculated by scientists; they are levels above which ecosystems are badly damaged. For ecosystems to survive, pollution must be kept below critical loads. Studies have shown that a 70 percent reduction in sulfur deposition is required to allow acid rain-damaged freshwater ecosystems in Great Britain to recover.

Acid snow

Acid does not only exist in rain, smog and dry deposition, it can also fall with snow. Polluted snow is filthy and grey. The snow holds the acid while the weather is cold, then when the weather warms there is a surge of acid as the snow melts. This can cause great damage to water life.

Forest damage

In many parts of the world, forests have suffered damage caused by acid rain and low-level ozone pollution. Acid rain has affected these pine needles (right). About one half of West Germany's forests are affected to some degree. Eastern Europe's forests are among the most damaged. In Britain, the New Forest and Epping Forest are among the worst affected areas. The San Bernadino Forest, near Los Angeles, has been badly harmed by ozone pollution, and many pine trees have died.

FACT FILE 2

Clean energy

One way of cutting down the pollution produced by power stations that burn fossil fuels (such as coal, oil, and gas) is to replace them with different types of power stations that emit much less or no pollution into the atmosphere. There is huge potential in the world for natural, clean energy, as these windmills on Orkney Island show. Many countries use hydroelectric power; the energy of water running downhill is harnessed to produce electricity. Nuclear power also cuts down the need to burn fossil fuels, although its use includes other risks. In the future, wind, waves and tides may be increasingly harnessed to produce clean energy.

Cleaning coal

Coal can be cleaned to minimize the amount of sulfur and nitrogen oxides it emits when it is burned. Various methods can be used to clean the coal, including crushing and washing it; the coal floats while the rest, including substances which contain sulfur, sinks.

Effects on fish

Trout and salmon are among the first fish to die when lakes and rivers become affected by acid rain. In 1900, fishermen caught 66,000 lb of salmon in the seven main rivers of southern Norway (shown in the print below), but since 1970 no salmon have been caught there.

GLOSSARY

Acid rain – rain which is acidic as a result of pollution. Along with acid rain comes a whole range of other types of pollution, including acid snow, smog, dry deposition and low-level ozone pollution.

Critical load – the estimated maximum level of pollution that an ecosystem can tolerate without suffering serious damage.

Ecosystem – a collection of living things and the environment they live in, which functions as a unit.

Global warming – the Earth's temperature varies naturally, warming and cooling over the ages. But when gases like carbon dioxide are put into the atmosphere, they increase the greenhouse effect. This may be causing global warming, and could ultimately have dramatic effects on climate all over the world.

Greenhouse effect – the warming process of the Earth's atmosphere. Some gases in the atmosphere allow energy from the Sun to pass through and warm the Earth's surface, and then trap the heat coming back. This keeps the atmosphere, and our planet, warm. The greenhouse effect helps make life on Earth possible.

Oxides of nitrogen – they are produced when fuels are burned, and also evaporate from the fertilizers that are used in large quantities in modern agriculture. They help form acid rain, turning into nitric acid in the atmosphere when they combine with water.

Oxides of sulfur – they are given off when fuels are burned, and contribute to the formation of acid rain, turning into sulfuric acid and sulfate in the atmosphere when they combine with water. The best known type is sulfur dioxide.

Ozone – a colorless gas which forms the ozone layer high in the atmosphere. This layer is vital to life on Earth as it protects our planet from the Sun's dangerous ultraviolet radiation. But ozone also occurs at ground level, being formed as sunlight strikes the pollution produced by vehicles. At ground level it is a type of pollution and causes damage to plants and people.

Pollution – when natural or human-made substances reach undesirable levels in the environment. Many pollutants occur naturally, such as from volcanoes, but at significantly lower levels.

INDEX

Photographic Credits:
Cover: Rex Features; pages 4, 7 top, 20 and 29 both: Bruce Coleman; pages 6 left, 7 bottom left, 15, 17 top, 18 and 22: The Environmental Picture Library; page 6 center: The Hutchison Library; pages 7 bottom center and bottom right and 25: The J.Allan Cash Library; pages 10, 11, 13 and 23: Robert Harding; pages 16 and 30 top: Planet Earth; page 17 bottom: Ivor Edmonds/ICCE Photolibrary; pages 19 and 21 bottom: Topham; page 24: Rex Features; page 30 bottom: Mary Evans Photo Library.